FISHING: TIPS & TECHNIQUES

SALTWATER FISHING

MARY-LANE KAM

rosen publishing's
rosen central

New York

For Ken Kamberg, my fishing buddy and so much more

Published in 2012 by The Rosen Publishing Group, Inc.
29 East 21st Street, New York, NY 10010

First Edition

Library of Congress Cataloging-in-Publication Data

Kamberg, Mary-Lane, 1948–
Saltwater fishing / Mary-Lane Kamberg.—1st ed.
    p. cm.—(Fishing: tips & techniques)
Includes bibliographical references and index.
ISBN 978-1-4488-4599-6 (library binding)
ISBN 978-1-4488-4608-5 (pbk.)
ISBN 978-1-4488-4739-6 (6-pack)
1. Saltwater fishing—Juvenile literature. I. Title.
SH457.K26 2012
799.16—dc22

2010050037

Manufactured in Malaysia

CPSIA Compliance Information: Batch #S11YA: For further information, contact Rosen Publishing, New York, New York, at 1-800-237-9932.

CONTENTS

*B*ait a hook. Drop a line. Catch a fish. For millions of anglers in the United States, that's a recipe for fun and relaxation. Just ask recreational anglers who fish the nation's rivers, lakes, and oceans.

Recreational fishing is also known as sport fishing or game fishing. These terms refer to all fishing, whether in freshwater or salt water. Saltwater and freshwater fishing are much the same, but there are some differences. Anglers fish at a faster pace in salt water. Marine fish grow much larger than freshwater fish, and most of them have teeth.

Saltwater fishing is full of action and excitement. There are many different kinds of fish to catch. Some of the most popular saltwater sport fish include marlin, sailfish, shark, halibut, cod, and tuna. These species make up only a small fraction of the 210,000 marine plants and animals known to science, according to the first Census of Marine Life.

The Census of Marine Life is a ten-year project completed in 2010 by a global network of researchers who collect information on ocean life. The project's goal was to learn how many different species of marine life exist, how many of each species there are, and where they live. They gathered this

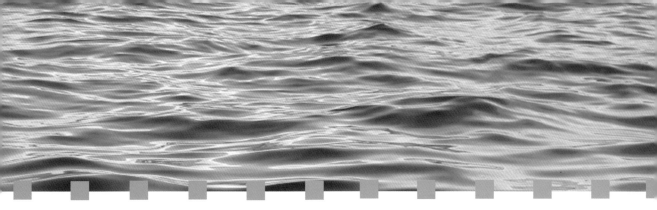

Saltwater fishing can be a fun family activity. Successful fishing involves following safety rules, using the right equipment and fishing methods, and following practices that preserve the environment.

information as the basis for future research. Scientists hope to track and measure the success of marine species both now and in the future. The Census of Marine Life created a database of species that includes nearly seventeen thousand known marine fish species.

According to the National Oceanic and Atmospheric Administration (NOAA), America has more than 12,383 miles (19,928.5 kilometers) of saltwater coastline. Counties in the United States that border an ocean represent only 17 percent of the nation's landmass. (That number does not include Alaska, which has 6,640 miles [10,686 km] of coastline.) Fifty-three percent of all Americans live within 50 miles (80.5 km) of a saltwater fishery. A fishery is an area where you can catch fish.

You can fish in salt water from land or sea. Saltwater sport fishing includes fishing from structures, beaches, or surf. You also can fish from boats—both close to the shore and out on the high seas. More than fifteen million Americans fish for fun in salt water, according to *Greenwire*, a leading source for news about energy and the environment. Saltwater sport fishing is a $31 billion industry in the United States.

This book will share the information that you need to know in order to enjoy recreational saltwater fishing. To participate in this sport, you must first learn safety and etiquette rules. You also need the right equipment. Rods, reels, and accessories are specialized: you need the right gear and bait to target specific types of fish in different conditions.

After reviewing some of your choices for gear, we'll discuss the many methods anglers use in salt water. For example, you can lower your bait to the bottom, or you can drag it behind a moving boat. Some anglers cast a line and reel it back in, hoping a nice fish will chase the bait and bite it.

Most saltwater fish species are fit for human consumption, and most anglers eat what they catch. So, you'll want to learn ways to prepare the fish you take home for cooking. This book will help with tips for the kitchen.

Many fisheries and species are threatened by commercial overfishing, overpopulation of one or more species, and poisons in the water. The last chapter reports on ways environmental groups and government agencies are working to identify, restore, and sustain fisheries. Find out what you can do to ensure that there will always be fish for anglers like you.

CHAPTER 1

SAFETY AND SPORTSMANSHIP

Spend a day in the sun along America's coastline. Head out for night fishing in a bay. Reel in a nice catch for dinner, and you've had a successful day.

However, nothing spoils an outing like mishaps or bad manners—not to mention an emergency. It is important to prepare in order to have an enjoyable saltwater fishing experience. You'll need to follow safety tips, sportsmanship rules, and fishing regulations carefully.

Be sure to obey all city, state, and federal laws for your location. You might need a fishing license or registration with the federal National Marine Fisheries Service. Be sure to carry all necessary papers. Observe size and catch limits, and be careful not to fish for species that are not permitted for the season. Following these practices makes you a responsible angler.

Keep your eye on the sky, even if you checked the forecast before setting out. Weather on the ocean can change quickly. Head for shore at the first sign of a storm.

Prepare for the Weather

Always check the weather forecast before going fishing. Wear appropriate clothing for the expected conditions. Take an extra set of dry clothes in a waterproof bag. In some areas you'll want to avoid red, yellow, or black clothing, which can attract gnats, black flies, and mosquitoes. Also, leave flip-flops at home. You'll need waders, wading shoes, or waterproof shoes or boots to remain stable for shore fishing or slippery boat decks.

Be ready for sun, wind, and water, as well as a sudden storm. Minimize the effects of a day in the sun by wearing a hat and sunglasses. Apply sunscreen, especially to the face. Be prepared for rain and thunderstorms, even if they are not in the forecast. Weather over the ocean changes quickly. If you need a rain jacket or windbreaker, wear one that fits loosely in the shoulders. That will give you room to handle your rod easily. Be sure to bring a well-stocked first-aid kit.

While boating, keep an eye on the sky. Watch for approaching thunderstorms. If your fishing rod buzzes, lightning may be about to strike. Crouch down and put your hands on your knees. If you see lightning or hear thunder, stop fishing. Immediately turn back to shore. Stay low in the boat. Regardless of the weather, never sit on the side of a boat or dangle your legs toward the water.

On the Water

If you use a boat, check wave height. Be sure the size of the boat is right for the conditions. The bigger the boat, the more stable it is in rough seas. The smaller the boat, the more likely you are to get seasick.

Seasickness, a type of motion sickness, can ruin a fishing trip. You might have nausea or feel tired or dizzy. You might sweat or get a headache. Worst of all, you might vomit. Children between the ages of two and twelve, women, and the elderly are more likely to suffer from seasickness. To prevent seasickness, watch your diet before the trip. Avoid a big meal of greasy food, bread, or pasta. Instead, chose a light meal that includes fruits, vegetables, and plenty of water.

On the boat, sit near the middle for the most stable ride. Some fishing boats have inside cabins. However, if you feel symptoms, stay in the fresh air. Focus your vision on the horizon. Some over-the-counter and prescription drugs, taken with adult guidance, can prevent or reduce symptoms of seasickness. However, some medicines work only if taken before setting out to sea.

Don't Rock the Boat!

Follow boating safety rules. Before you leave, tell someone where you will be fishing and when you'll be back. Describe the boat. Ask your friend to call the U.S. Coast Guard if your return is long overdue.

Obey the requirements on the boat manufacturer's capacity plate. This plate tells the number of people and weight allowed on the boat. Balance the weight of people and gear evenly throughout the boat. Otherwise, the boat could capsize, or overturn.

Safe operation of a boat depends on the condition of the driver. According to the U.S. Coast Guard, alcohol use is involved in almost one-third of all recreational boating deaths. Boating under the influence of alcohol or other drugs is just as illegal as driving a car under the influence. The U.S. Coast Guard and all states define legal limits for alcohol use in their waters. They are comparable to limits for driving motor vehicles. Passengers under the influence also risk dangerous falls overboard. Never board a boat if the operator or any passenger has been using alcohol or other drugs. Discourage alcohol use while underway.

Wearing a life jacket is an important way to ensure your safety when boating. If you have an emergency, contact the U.S. Coast Guard for rescue.

Good Sportsmanship

With the popularity of sport fishing, anglers must often share the water. Fishing etiquette calls for respecting other anglers. Lend a hand if others ask for help. If another person loses an item in the water, help retrieve it if you can do so safely. Offer to tow a boat with a disabled motor. Give directions. Lend extra line or other equipment.

Safety First

The ocean poses dangers, even close to shore. Always go fishing with someone else. If an emergency occurs, your buddy can rescue you or call for help.

The first rule for shore fishing is: Never turn your back on the ocean. A sudden high wave can knock you off your footing. The impact can also cause head, neck, or spine injuries similar to the whiplash experienced in a rear-end car accident. To some, facing the ocean is also a way to show respect for its awesome power.

If you spend time around water, knowing how to swim is important. Even if you can do the backstroke, you still need water safety and rescue skills appropriate for fishing and boating.

You always need a personal flotation device when fishing from a boat. Many people who have drowned in boating accidents might have lived if they had worn life jackets. Choose one approved by the U.S. Coast Guard, and be sure it fits correctly.

Also, be sure to bring at least two forms of communication equipment with you when boating. Then you can contact someone if you are in trouble and get help much more quickly. Useful items include a cell phone, hand-held waterproof radio, personal emergency locator beacon, and red flares. A sound signal, such as a horn, can also be helpful.

If your buddy falls into the water, resist the urge to jump in after him or her unless you are a certified lifeguard. Instead, extend a pole or rope, or toss a life preserver or boat cushion. The American Red Cross and other groups include such skills in their lesson programs.

Share knowledge of fishing techniques, habitat, or behavior with less experienced fishers who are eager to learn. Most important, render aid or call emergency services when needed.

Another important rule of good sportsmanship is to stay quiet. Loud voices, music, barking dogs, or other loud noises scare away fish and disturb others who are fishing. In addition, it is a courtesy to move on to another place if someone is already fishing a spot. If that's where you want to fish, come back later after the other angler leaves. If you are in a boat, stay away from anglers who are fishing from the shore. Also stay away from other boats already working an area, whether they are at anchor or moving as they fish.

If you are part of a fishing party aboard a boat, place your rod in a holder to save your spot. Never move another angler's rod from its holder without permission. In general, respect other anglers' property. Also respect property owners' rights if you must cross private land to get to the place where you want to fish.

Give fellow anglers a fair chance to catch fish. Don't crowd fishing buddies or strangers. Keep your fishing line clear of others' lines so that they don't get tangled. If someone hooks a fish, keep your own line out of the way so that the angler can bring in the catch.

Always look behind you and to both sides before casting so that you don't endanger others. You don't want your hook to injure someone's eye or skin. Never cast toward another person or over his or her head. If you or another angler gets a hook caught in the skin, there is an appropriate way to take it out. Carefully push the point of the hook forward through the skin. Cut off the barb on the end. Then pull the rest of the hook back through, the way it came in.

Fishing boat operators should quickly launch and pull their boats out of the water. Move away from the boat ramp to load and unload food, drink, and fishing gear so that others don't have to wait to use the ramp.

When leaving shore, boaters keep red buoys to their left, but they keep them to the right as they return to the harbor. The saying "Red, right, returning" helps boaters remember.

Finding Your Way

The Coast Guard and the U.S. Army Corps of Engineers install and maintain a system of buoys (also called channel markers) to help boaters safely navigate federal waters. All boats use the system to help sea traffic run smoothly.

Knowing the colors and shapes of the various buoys helps boat operators follow the rules and take the correct course in the water. This helps prevent collisions and other trouble. For example, large boats operating near coastlines risk running aground or getting stuck in the

When boating, be sure you understand and obey signs marking no-wake zones and speed limits. These signs help boat traffic navigate smoothly.

sand if they enter water that is too shallow. Reefs, underwater wrecks, and other hazards also pose dangers to fishing boats.

Red and green buoys tell boat operators which part of a waterway to use, depending on where they are headed. A saying familiar to sailors is "Red, right, returning." That means if you are coming into a harbor, keep the red buoys on your right. When you are leaving the harbor, keep the green ones on your right. Red channel markers are shaped like triangles with the pointed end up. Green ones are shaped like rectangles. Floating red buoys are called nuns, and floating green ones are called cans. Buoys often have lights with the same colors so that boaters can follow them at night or in fog.

Additional colors and shapes of buoys indicate such information as safe water and locations of pipelines, fish trap areas, and other features. Buoys are marked on nautical charts, which all boating anglers need on board.

Obey no-wake zones, speed limits, and rules about areas where you can and cannot operate a boat. Wake is the path of waves created by the movement of the boat. Signs that say "No Wake" mean you should slow down to protect property, docked boats, or wildlife from damage from big waves. Also slow your speed in foul weather and around smaller boats so that you don't rock them with your wake.

CHAPTER 2

GEARING UP

Saltwater fishing equipment must match your prey. Saltwater fish are stronger and fight harder than freshwater fish of the same size. So, saltwater gear must be stronger than gear for freshwater. Also, the salt in sea water damages freshwater equipment. You need salt-resistant gear for ocean fishing.

Rods and Reels

It's easy to recognize a saltwater rod. There are two places to hold it. Hold the grip above the reel to set the hook. Use the grip below the reel to support the rod as you land the fish. Compare rods according to length, weight, and flexibility. Long rods cast farthest, but you need more physical strength to cast them than shorter ones.

It's important to use fishing gear designed for salt water. A saltwater rod has two places to grip—one for setting the hook and one to support the rod as you land the fish.

Shorter rods are easier to handle and store. If you're a beginner, start with a spinning rod that measures 6 to 7 feet (1.8 to 2.1 meters) long; it will work for most saltwater species. You can add new rods as your needs and experience change.

Reels hold, release, and roll up fishing line. Revolving-spool reels roll to unwind line. They can handle heavy line, but they are subject to backlash. Backlash is tangled line that occurs when the line is reeled out too quickly. Fixed-spool reels let out line from a stationary spool. They are less likely to tangle the line. Not every reel works with every rod. You need to match your reel to your rod. The best bet is a rod and reel packaged together by the manufacturer.

Hooks, Lines, and Sinkers

You don't know which fish might head your way, so buy a variety of hooks. Match the size of the hook to the size of your bait and the kind of fish you are trying to catch. For natural bait, use a circle hook or a J hook. A circle hook will not catch in a fish's stomach. If a fish swallows it, it rolls back into the mouth and catches there. A circle hook is also easy to remove. A J hook is commonly used as well, but a fish can swallow this hook and it can be hard to remove. Some artificial baits, called lures, use treble hooks. A treble hook is one with three hooks on the same stem. You have a better chance of catching a fish with this hook. But be careful not to hook yourself while working with one.

Choose line that is built for the task of reeling in the size fish you want. Line is rated according to strength. Breaking strength is the number of pounds or kilograms of weight the line can hold without breaking. A 20-pound (9.1 kilograms) test line, for example, can hold 20 pounds (9.1 kg) without breaking. Thickness helps determine strength. Thick line is usually stronger than thin line. However, thinner line can

Lures are artificial baits that resemble a sport fish's natural foods—usually smaller fish, shrimp, or other marine species.

be harder for fish to see. Some kinds of fish, such as bream, will not bite if they see the line. These fish are called line shy.

Monofilament line is the most popular type of fishing line. Made from a single strand of nylon, it is good for casting. It comes in a wide selection of strengths, from 1-pound (0.45 kg) weight to more than 200-pound (90.7 kg) weight. Braided line has several strands of fiber. It is best for reef fishing because corals can fray single-strand line. Line for deepwater trolling is made from wire.

You also need sinkers, swivels, and snaps. Sinkers are metal weights that keep the hook and bait from floating on the surface. Swivels and snaps tie to the end of the line. Swivels prevent twisted line. Snaps make changing hooks easy.

Baiting the Hook

Natural baits are usually called bait, while artificial baits are called lures. Many saltwater anglers—and the game fish they are seeking—prefer natural bait. But lures can catch lots of fish, too.

Live small fish make popular bait. Use pilchards to catch snappers and other small to medium-size fish. Pinfish are somewhat bigger and

Instead of buying live bait, catch your own using a casting net. Throw it so it spreads out over the water. Weights along the edge will cause the net to sink and trap small fish.

tempt larger fish. Use small mullets, called finger mullets, for small sport fish. You can use 2-pounders (0.9 kg) for big game fish.

Another popular bait is menhaden, a marine fish also known as shad, pogy, or bunker. Recreational anglers use it while bottom fishing to attract such fish as striped bass, weakfish, and mackerel. Saltwater anglers also use shrimp, crab, and even worms.

Chum is natural bait made of fish that is ground like hamburger. Chum is held in a net bag or wire cage and dragged behind a boat to attract fish to the area. Blood and fish oil from the chum create a slick on the water. Chum is not bait in the sense of being dangled from a hook. You still need a hook with bait or a lure.

You can buy natural baits in bait shops or tackle stores. You can also catch them yourself with a cast net or sabiki rig. A cast net has weighted edges. Throw it so that it spreads across the surface and sinks. With luck, it will be full of baitfish when you pull it in. A sabiki rig attaches to line on a sabiki rod and reel. The rig has six hooks, each with a small, colorful bead. Often, the beads are neon pink or green.

It's a Fake!

Game fish are attracted to motion, shapes, colors, smells, and even sounds. Lures appeal to these senses. Lures are artificial baits with hooks attached. They are made from such materials as wood, metal, plastic, glass, fur, feathers, and rubber. Some examples of lures include flies, spoons, spinners, plugs, poppers, and soft baits.

Saltwater flies are lightweight lures, which are tied to hooks to attract fish. They are designed to look like small fish, crustaceans, insects, and other marine animals as they move through the water. Use them with a fly rod and heavy line. Some flies land softly on the surface, and others are designed to move underwater.

An angler shops for artificial flies to tie onto his hooks. Made of feathers, fur, thread, or other materials, flies resemble baitfish or other aquatic prey.

Metal lures called spoons and spinners attract fish with movement and reflection. The silver or gold spoons and spinner blades reflect sunlight, which attracts fish. Spoons usually have oval shapes. They wobble through water. Spinners spin. They have blades that rotate in circles.

A plug is a wooden or plastic lure shaped and painted to look like a small fish. Manufactured plugs are engineered, painted, and tested to imitate small baitfish. Some plugs, called poppers, make a loud popping or buzzing sound. They attract game fish with noise.

Safe Storage and Care of Gear

Store sharp items, such as hooks, lures, gaffs, and knives, when they are not in use. On shore, keep small items in a tackle box. On a boat, choose places where a sudden tip of the boat won't send them flying. Store hooks and lures in a closed tackle box. Always keep your rod in a holder or locker so that no one will trip over it.

After fishing, clean your equipment to prevent saltwater damage. Rinse your rod and reel with fresh water. When the season ends, separate the rod and reel. Soak the rod in soapy water, and remove any salt deposits with a soft brush.

At the end of the season, you'll need to throw away about 75 percent of the line from the reel. Rinse the reel in fresh water and let it dry. Follow the manufacturer's directions to clean and lubricate all moving parts. Add new line. Store in a padded container in a cool, dry place.

Saltwater plugs are easy to lose or wear out. Fish that break your line steal your plugs. Also, salt water ruins paint and rusts hooks.

Soft baits are soft, flexible plastic lures. They look like shrimp, crabs, small fish, or worms. Some manufacturers add fishy scents to soft bait to appeal to a game fish's strong sense of smell. Store soft baits away from other lures. The chemicals used to make them can ruin hard plastic lures and paint finishes.

Landing Fish

Gear for landing a fish or getting it into a boat includes leaders, landing nets, and gaffs. A leader is a wire or monofilament line that connects fishing line to the hook. The leader is heavier than the line in order to handle the weight of the fish. For example, you might pair a 20-pound (9.1 kg) test line with a 100-pound (45.4 kg) test leader.

Landing nets let you scoop fish from the water. Nets are made of twine, nylon, rubber, monofilament net, or neoprene. Neoprene is a synthetic rubber, which causes the least harm to fish. A gaff is a big hook. Use it to grasp a heavy fish and lift it into the boat.

For large game fish, you need a long-handled gaff to bring your catch into the boat if you plan to eat it. Never gaff a fish you plan to release.

A few more basics are all you need. Take a toenail clipper to cut line. A pair of rustproof needle-nose pliers comes in handy for unhooking fish and other tasks. You also need an assortment of knives.

Great Gadgets

Some great gadgets can help you catch fish. Depth finders, fish finders, and global positioning systems are items you might want to try.

Depth finders are navigational instruments. They use either radar or sound waves to tell how deep water is. Some models show pictures of

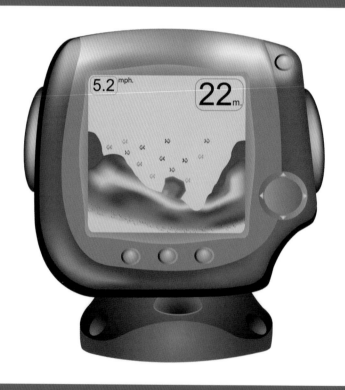

Gadgets like this fish finder show anglers where fish are located and how deep they are swimming.

the ocean floor. A fish finder uses radar to determine the location of fish and the depth at which they are swimming. Some fish finders measure surface temperature. Others include speed sensors. You can also choose LCD or color screens. Color screens have better images, but they are more expensive. A global positioning system (GPS) uses satellites to pinpoint places on Earth. It tells boaters where they are located. It also helps them return to favorite fishing spots.

While electronic gadgets are fun to have and use, some cost a lot of money. Watch your budget. You may get more pleasure—and catch more fish—by investing in a better quality rod and reel. Remember, people have been catching fish for thousands of years. Fishermen were successful even without these high-tech gadgets.

CHAPTER 3

SALTWATER FISHING METHODS

ike humans, fish have the senses of sight, smell, taste, hearing, and touch. To catch fish, appeal to one or more of these senses. Fish are always looking for food, so the key is to put your bait or lure where they are looking. Some fish are bottom feeders. Others hide in structures and wait for prey to swim by. Still others chase down their food. Different fishing techniques have developed to catch saltwater prey where they live and feed.

Popular Fishing Methods

Some popular types of saltwater fishing include bottom fishing, trolling, structure fishing, jetty fishing, float fishing, surf fishing, jigging, still fishing, fly fishing, and spear fishing.

Bottom fishing is one of the most popular fishing techniques in salt water. With

Trolling behind a moving powerboat is popular for offshore fishing of such big sport fish as tuna and marlin. Close to shore, the method is used for kingfish, bluefish, and jacks.

this method, the hook is suspended 1 or 2 feet (0.3 or 0.6 m) from the ocean floor. You can bottom fish from a dock, pier, beach, or surf. You can also use this method from a boat, especially near coral, artificial reefs, or underwater structures like sunken ships.

Trolling is another common fishing method in salt water, especially in the open ocean. The fisher puts bait or a lure in the water and drags it behind a powerboat. Use trolling for billfish, sailfish, tuna, and marlin. You can also use it closer to shore for kingfish, bluefish, and jacks. Some anglers use chum to attract fish to their boats when trolling. Drift fishing is similar to trolling, except that you "go with the flow" without a powered motor.

Structure fishing is popular for fishing from piers, docks, bridges, and other structures. The most commonly fished structure is a jetty. A jetty is a barrier made of rocks, concrete, wood, or rubble that sticks out into a body of water. To fish, you walk the length of the jetty. It's uneven and slippery, so you need safety footwear called jetty creepers.

You can stand on the beach or wade out from shore for surf fishing. To avoid injury from a sudden wave, never turn your back on the ocean.

Float fishing is a method that uses a bobber or other floating device. The device stays on top of the water. A sinker attached to the line keeps the bait under water. The float controls the depth of the hook. When the bobber dips under water, you have likely hooked a fish.

Surf fishing is done from a beach or by wading out from shore. Fresh bait is preferred, but you can use metal lures, especially plugs. Some popular surf fishing targets include striped bass, bluefish, weakfish, red drum, and snook.

In still fishing, you keep bait in the water as you fish from a pier, bridge, or anchored boat. Still fishing is a good way to catch giant sea bass, rockfish, and barracuda. If you are using a lure, try jigging. Drop in the lure. Then jerk it back to the surface. The movement gets the attention of such fish as grunts and black sea bass.

Fly fishing uses a rod to cast lightweight flies on heavy line. You hold the line across your palm and fingers instead of on a reel. Fly fishing is among the least common types of fishing in salt water, but its popularity is growing. Fly fishing usually occurs close to shore. However, such species as sailfish, marlin, and Pacific bluefish have been caught in the open ocean with fly fishing gear.

Underwater Fishing

Spear fishing is an underwater sport that uses a speargun instead of a rod and reel. A speargun is used to fire a spear that strikes the fish.

The fisher can hunt by free diving, snorkeling, or scuba diving. Free diving is simply holding your breath under water. Snorkeling is swimming using swim fins and a diving mask equipped with a breathing tube. "Scuba" stands for "self-contained underwater breathing apparatus." In this form of diving, a container of compressed air allows you to stay under water for longer periods of time and reach greater depths.

You can fish by diving from the shore or from a boat. When boats are present, use a buoy tied to the speargun to warn others that you are underwater. Spear fishing is particularly popular in Hawaii. It is legal in most states. However, in many areas, you are restricted to hunting certain species. There are also regulations about the type of power the spear gun uses. Spear guns are dangerous weapons. Never shoot one toward another person, dock, campsite, or boat ramp.

When to Fish

The best time to fish depends on the type of fish you seek and their habits and habitat. Off the South Carolina coast, for example, spring

A breathing tube allowed this fisher to snorkel just under the ocean surface, keeping his eyes on the prize: a Hawaiian parrot fish caught with a speargun instead of a rod and reel.

and fall are the best times for fishing near the coast. Food for game fish is plentiful then.

Many game fish eat young fish, called fry. For example, halibut and calico bass like Pacific surfperch fry. Both of these sport fishes usually swim in deeper water. However, they will come closer to shore when the surfperch grow to about two inches (five centimeters) long. Along America's West Coast, that happens between March and July. That's a good time to fish for halibut and calico bass in the Pacific.

If you are surf fishing, you'll have better luck in the early morning or late evening when the tide is coming in or going out. The water

Structure fishing from a pier can have good results close to shore, especially at night, when lights attract fish to the area.

currents carry the shrimp, small crabs, and baitfish that bigger fish eat. These baitfish have difficulty controlling their movement in strong currents, so they are easier for bigger fish to feed on. Start fishing an hour or two before each change in tide and continue for up to an hour afterward. For boat fishing at these times of day, drop your bait near the tide line. The tide line is the front edge of the moving water, whichever direction it flows.

The Two B's

Use the two B's to look for fish: bait and birds. You can usually find fish near one or both. Drop your line where your prey finds its favorite food. Also, watch for seabirds. They often eat the same foods that fish like. If you see birds, sport fish may be feeding in the same area. Birds may hover over an area or peck in wet sand. In southern California, for example, birds called sandpipers eat sand crabs. So do such fish as corbina and barred surfperch. If you see the birds digging, you are likely to find the fish in nearby water.

Sometimes, you can find game fish by scanning the surface for light reflecting off fins or tails. Fish on the move may break the surface or disturb it. Watch for moving water in the shape of a V. Or, look for a series of ripples called nervous water moving on the surface.

Pier fishing is best at night. Small fish swim in toward the lights, and larger fish soon follow. For sharks, you'll have better luck fishing after the sun goes down. They are more active at night. In fact, most species, including snapper, feed at night. You can fish for many species during the first five hours after sundown. Be sure you have flashlights so that you can see what you're doing! Successful night fishing often depends on attracting fish to movement or smell. Chumming is a good method to use when night fishing by boat.

Where to Fish

You can use most fishing methods in each of the three main locations for saltwater fishing: shore, inshore, and offshore. Shore fishing includes fishing from a beach, pier, jetty, rock formation, or other coastal feature. Inshore fishing occurs within sight of the coastline. It includes fishing in relatively shallow water in a bay that leads to the open ocean. Offshore fishing, or deep-sea fishing, occurs in the open ocean. This is the place to go for big sport fish. When going offshore, many anglers take a party boat for drift fishing or a charter boat that offers drift fishing along with trolling and bottom fishing.

You'll find fish where they hide or hunt. The more you know about fish behavior and habitats, the easier it will be to find the best places to drop or cast your line. Knowing coastal features and the composition of the ocean floor in your area will help you know where to fish. If you find the game fish's food, the larger fish you are seeking are likely lurking nearby.

Some fish hide in stands of kelp, near coral reefs, or in shipwrecks. For instance, you'll find grouper and snapper near coral reefs, waiting for prey to swim by. That's where you'll want to drop your bait. Other fish chase their food. Some small fish hide under piers and eat organisms that attach themselves to the structure. Game fish swim under the pier

Coral reefs support many species of marine life, especially sport fish and the smaller fish they feed on. Take care to protect the reefs from damage.

looking for a good meal. At sea, look for strong ocean currents, which carry small fish and shrimp. That's where to look for larger fish that eat these species.

Learn about habitats of baitfish and other marine organisms such as crabs, mussels, and clam worms. For example, in Northeastern states, bluefish, striped bass, and bonito usually swim too far from shore for surf fishing. However, you can catch them from the beach when sand eels are around. (Sand eels favor shorelines with soft sand or mud bottoms.)

Water temperature also affects where different species swim. Shallow water is usually warmer than deep water. Water closer to the surface is warmer than deeper water in the same place. Also consider the season and latitude where you are fishing. Latitude is the distance north or south of the equator. Fish in warmer waters for sailfish, marlin, and tiger sharks. Fish in cold water for cod and Atlantic mackerel.

CHAPTER 4

HANDLING THE CATCH

What do you do after you catch a fish? Before you land it or bring it into the boat, make a decision. Are you going to eat it or let it go?

Let It Go? You Just Caught It!

No matter when or where you fish, you will not want to harvest every fish you catch. The fish you catch may be too small, or the species may be spawning, endangered, or out of season. Perhaps you've already caught the legal limit for the day. In some cases, regulations require release of certain species. In Florida, for example, anglers cannot keep goliath or Nassau grouper. The harvesting of snook, red drum, and spotted sea trout is limited to certain sizes and times of the year. These kinds of conservation efforts have restored or sustained some fish species in Florida and other states.

Catch-and-Release Fishing

Catching fish and letting them go is called catch-and-release fishing. Some anglers enjoy the challenge of catching fish but release all the fish they catch. Others practice catch-and-release fishing only in certain circumstances. Critics of the practice say being caught and released—only

You won't want to keep every fish you catch. If you're going to release a fish, keep it in the water. Support the fish horizontally and gently remove the hook.

to be hooked again—is cruel to fish. However, it is one way to ensure that fish grow to adulthood and reproduce. That means more fish for future anglers.

If you are going to release a fish, do your best to ensure its survival. Use equipment and methods to protect the fish. For instance, use circle hooks or hooks without barbs for catch-and-release fishing.

The two main reasons a released fish dies are stress and injury. Physical stress from fighting disrupts a fish's metabolism. Metabolism refers to the body's chemical processes. If you release the fish right away, the imbalance soon returns to normal. However, a long fight can exhaust a fish. It may not recover. To keep stress to a minimum, use tackle strong enough to reel in the fish as quickly as possible. Decide whether to keep or release a hooked fish before taking it out of the water.

What Is Venting?

Bringing a fish from deep to shallow water too quickly stresses it. This can happen with reef fishing. Excess gas collects in the fish's body. A fish in trouble has bulging eyes or a bloated belly. Sometimes, its stomach sticks out of its mouth. Before letting the fish go, release the excess gas. Venting is the way to do that.

Since 2008, federal regulations have required that anglers carry a venting tool when fishing reefs in the Gulf of Mexico. For venting, a fisher can use a 16-gauge needle stuck in a block of wood or a syringe without the plunger. One can also use a manufactured venting tool. (Never use a knife or an ice pick.)

Place the point of the venting tool under a scale, about 2 inches (5 cm) behind the base of a pectoral fin. Pectoral fins lie just behind the gill openings. Gills are breathing organs. They are found on each side of the fish, just behind the head. Gently insert the needle a short way into the body cavity. Gases will escape. Then you can safely release the fish. Never puncture an inverted stomach or shove it back into the fish's mouth. The stomach will go back where it belongs once you release the fish.

Preventing Harm

Prevent harm to the fish from the hook or improper handling. If possible, remove the hook while the fish is still in the water. If the fish has swallowed the hook, leave the hook alone. Snip the line as close to the hook as possible. Over time, most hooks dissolve. The fish will survive.

When lifting a fish that you may release, use a landing net to protect it.

Avoid stainless-steel hooks. They won't dissolve and are outlawed in some areas.

If you intend to release a fish, do not lift it directly from the water to the boat. Instead, use a landing net. Never gaff a fish you intend to release unless you can gaff it through the lower jaw. If you must handle a fish, use wet hands and support the fish horizontally.

Trophy Fish

Whether you choose to eat or release your catch, you might want to record the event. You can keep the memory with a photograph, video, or fiberglass model.

For a photograph, choose a background without buckets, coolers, and other gear. Take off sunglasses and hats that cast shadows on the face. Keep the fish wet. It will show up better. Hold it by supporting it horizontally.

Camcorders, cell phone cameras, and other video equipment can also help you remember your fishing trip. For underwater activities like speargun fishing, use a waterproof camcorder case, an underwater camcorder, or a high-definition recorder.

A taxidermist is a person who mounts fish and other animals for display. Today, taxidermists design fiberglass models. If you'd like to mount a fish this way, take several color pictures. Weigh it and carefully measure its dimensions. Make careful notes about outstanding characteristics. Your model will look like the real thing.

Don't touch its gills or eyes, and don't hold it by the jaw. It could lose its ability to feed—and then starve. Gently release the fish headfirst.

Cleaning Fish

Fish is low in calories, high in protein, and low in saturated fat. Fish oil is a good source of omega-3 fatty acids, especially from saltwater species such as tuna, herring, and mackerel. Omega-3 fatty acids are important for children's growth and development. They also lower the risk of heart disease and other ailments.

To fillet a fish, use a long, thin knife with a flexible blade to separate the bones from the flesh and skin.

If you plan to eat your catch, keep the fish cold and clean it as soon as possible. If you can't clean it immediately after catching it, keep it cold and wet until you can. Another option is to keep the fish alive in a live well or a basket kept in the water. Observe fish cleaning rules and regulations for the area. Some places ban fish cleaning on boats or beaches. Many marinas and boat-launch areas have fish cleaning stations for anglers to use.

You will need a scaling knife, pocketknife, and fillet knife for cleaning fish. Be sure to get an adult's permission and supervision before using these tools. A scaling knife has a dull blade. It removes scales when you clean your catch. Use a pocketknife or other sharp knife with a relatively short blade to remove a fish's internal organs. A fillet knife has a long, narrow, flexible blade. Use it to separate flesh from bone.

There are two main methods of cleaning fish: gutting them (removing the scales and internal organs) and filleting them. Filleting separates the flesh from the bones and sometimes the skin.

If the fish has scales, use a scaling knife to remove them. Lay the fish on its side, perpendicular to your body. Hold it by the tail. Place the knife edge against the tail end of the fish at a 45-degree angle (about half of a square corner). Face the blade toward you. Stroke the blade away from you toward the head. Move the blade against the direction of the scales. Scaling is a messy job. Do it outside if you can. If inside, keep the fish in a tub or sink full of water while you scale it.

To gut a fish, use a pocketknife or other sharp knife with a short blade. Lay the fish on its side or back. Insert the knife, with the blade facing out, at the end of the fish. Pull the blade through the belly skin and toward the head, all the way to the gills. Remove the internal organs and gills, including any small bones. Leave the fins in place. You can easily remove them after cooking. If you want to remove the head, cut just behind the pectoral fins, from the top down.

To have an old-fashioned fish fry like this one in Virginia, serve breaded fish fried in hot oil. Grilled and broiled fish are healthier choices to eat regularly.

To fillet a fish, use a fillet knife. Slice the length of the fish's back down to the backbone. Leaving the rib cage intact, follow the curve of the rib cage with the blade. If you want to remove the skin, use a sawing motion. Trim any excess fat.

After cleaning fish, chill immediately to keep fish fresh. Use a cooler of ice, or put fish in a slurry. A slurry is a thin mixture of water and other material. Try mixing seawater with saltwater ice. The salt makes the water-and-ice mixture colder than ice made with fresh water.

Cooking Fish

For many anglers, the best part of a fishing trip is the old-fashioned fish fry that follows. Frying is a popular method for cooking fish. Dip the fish in a mixture of milk and beaten eggs. Then drag it through breadcrumbs. Fry it in vegetable oil in a frying pan or deep fryer. It tastes good! However, frying is not the healthiest way to cook fish. Frying increases the fish's fat and calorie content. For a healthier meal, grill or broil fish so that the fat drips away from the flesh.

The best time to cook fish is right after it is caught. The second-best time is within a few hours. Freeze what you can't cook, and eat that soon. To save fish for another occasion, tightly wrap the gutted fish in plastic wrap. Then cover with heavy aluminum foil, tape the package shut, and freeze. Place fish fillets in a resealable freezer bag. Cover the fillets with fresh water. Carefully press out any air and seal the bag. Label with the type of fish and the date before placing the bag in the freezer. Frozen fish keep for up to two months.

CHAPTER 5

FISHING AND THE ENVIRONMENT

Fisheries around the world are in trouble. In some areas, anglers and commercial fishers have taken too many of a particular species. In many cases, the populations of those species have decreased faster than they can reproduce. In other fisheries, too many of a particular species threaten other species. Pesticides, methylmercury, industrial waste, and other pollutants have contaminated seawater in many places. Habitat destruction and bad fishing practices threaten many species of both baitfish and sport fish.

Protecting Fish Species

In 2010, efforts were underway to protect the Atlantic bluefin tuna under the U.S. Endangered Species Act. According to the Center for Biological Diversity, overfishing of the tuna has caused an 80 percent decline in its population from what would be expected without fishing. The center also said that in 2007, sport anglers reported catches of 34,514 tons (31,311 metric tons) of eastern Atlantic bluefin tuna. The amount was over 5,000 tons (4,536 metric tons) more than that allowed for sport fishers. The species is popular for sushi and other dishes, so sport anglers may have sold their catches. Usually, commercial fishers sell tuna. In fact, most sport anglers consider selling the fish unethical. However, environmentalists said that the recreational count was too low. They estimated the number to be twice what was reported.

Conservationists worry about species on the decline. However, the Atlantic swordfish population made a comeback in 2010. Overfishing in

Bluefin tuna is prized for its fatty belly flesh, but overfishing has caused an enormous decline in its population. International efforts to protect the species have failed so far.

the early 1990s had severely reduced the swordfish population. Action taken at that time by environmental organizations and the National Marine Fisheries Service restored the species.

Sometimes, groups encourage taking a specific species. In 2010, an invasion of lionfish threatened coral reef fisheries along the East Coast, Florida Keys, and Gulf of Mexico. According to NOAA, the number of lionfish grew by 700 percent between 2004 and 2008. Lionfish eat many colorful fish that populate coral reefs. For example, they eat parrot fish, which eat algae on the reefs and keep the reefs clean. Reduced reef fish populations also include juvenile snapper and grouper sport fish. These effects can, in turn, reduce the number of tourists who come to fish, snorkel, and scuba dive in these areas. A reduction in tourism affects the economy in a negative way.

Humans may be the only predator that can stop the lionfish explosion. Lionfish are eaten as a delicacy in the Far East. So, conservationists in the United States are working with restaurant chefs to create recipes for lionfish. They hope this action will encourage catching, cooking, and eating the species. If the plan works, the number of lionfish will decrease. Then the coral reefs, and the variety of life among them, can be restored, sustained, or increased.

Protecting Fishing Areas

Along with protecting fish, conservationists seek to protect saltwater fishing areas. In central California, for example, all human activity is banned in designated marine protected areas. The areas, most of which cover less than 1.5 square miles (3.9 square kilometers), are like state and national parks. The idea is to give these parts of the ocean a rest so that the water, plants, and animals can recover and thrive. The effort has had positive results. Fish in these reserves grow larger and produce more offspring than those in unprotected parts of the ocean.

Oil spills and other severe pollution threaten fisheries. On April 20, 2010, an explosion and fire on the Deepwater Horizon oil-drilling rig killed eleven men. The rig, which operated near Louisiana in the Gulf of Mexico, was licensed to BP, a global energy group once known as British Petroleum. Millions of gallons of oil poured into the water. Oil is hazardous to fish. Some worried that the dispersants—chemicals used to break up and scatter oil—were just as bad.

On June 2, 2010, the U.S. government restricted or closed fishing in 37 percent of federal waters in the Gulf. The NOAA and the U.S. Food and Drug Administration

An oil-covered fish floats off the Louisiana coast three days after the Deep Horizon oil spill in 2010. It may take decades for the Gulf of Mexico to cleanse itself completely.

(FDA) worked together to test samples of Gulf species for signs of contamination. By late October 2010, much of the area had been reopened to fishing. About 4 percent of the Gulf's federal waters, or 9,444 square miles (24,461 sq km), remained closed, according to the National Marine Fisheries Service.

Licensing and Regulation

Federal, state, and local governments hope to manage fisheries to ensure that there will always be plenty of fish. They address these kinds of issues with laws, regulations, and license requirements. Federal waters extend 200 miles (321.9 km) from the 3-mile (4.8 km) limit where state waters end. In 2006, the Magnuson-Stevens Act created registration requirements for saltwater anglers. Federal regulators are creating a database to better track the number of people fishing and how much fishing they are doing. Beginning in 2011, the National Marine Fisheries Service will charge a fee up to $25 for anglers who must register. Saltwater anglers under the age of sixteen do not need to register.

Also, anglers do not have to register and pay the fee if their state already has a registry or licensing program for recreational saltwater fishing. People on state registries are automatically included on the national list. However, as 2010 came to an end, legislators in such states as Florida, New Jersey, Maine, Maryland, Rhode Island, and Texas were still debating the issue. Some wanted to set up their own state registries. Others wanted to require licenses or fees for saltwater fishing in addition to their freshwater fishing licenses. Many said that they didn't want to license or charge fees at all for fishing in the open ocean. Anglers in states that have not addressed the issue by the 2011 deadline must join the national registry and pay the federal fee. To determine if you need to register with the National Saltwater Angler Registry, go to https://www.countmyfish.noaa.gov.

Is Eating Fish Risky?

Most saltwater fish contain traces of methylmercury. Methylmercury is a compound of mercury and carbon that is dangerous to living things. It accumulates in living organisms instead of being released as waste. Some fish contain high levels of this compound. Large fish and fish that have lived a long time have the most. Other contaminants in saltwater fish include pesticides and industrial waste. In fish, contaminants concentrate in the skin and fat.

Cooking cannot remove toxins. You can avoid problems by varying your sources of protein. Eat different kinds of fish during a given week or month. Check with your local health department or fishing authorities to learn which species in your area to limit or avoid. Young children and pregnant women are more sensitive to contaminants than others, so they should stick to low-risk fish. Fortunately, kid favorites like fish sticks and restaurant fish sandwiches are usually made from low-risk species.

State governments also manage saltwater resources in many coastal areas. States can determine the size and number of species that you can harvest. They impose fishing seasons by species. These seasons protect fish during the periods that they spawn, hatch, and grow to adulthood. They also govern gear and fishing methods by species.

Regulations vary by state. For instance, some states require fishing licenses for saltwater fishing, while other states do not. Some states set a minimum age for operating watercraft. Some require an approved boating education course. State regulations usually come from state agencies that deal with conservation, natural resources, fish, or wildlife.

Look for rules for your area by contacting the appropriate agency. Do an Internet search for "fishing regulations" and the state where you want to fish.

What You Can Do

You can help care for beaches, oceans, and fisheries. First, leave the beach cleaner than you found it. Pick up litter left by others, as well as your own trash. Carry out everything you brought to the beach, especially used fishing line and old or broken tackle. However, never remove seaweed, driftwood, or other natural items that provide food, habitat, or shelter for animals that live there. Stick to paths and walkways when walking near sand dunes. When boating, keep your trash onboard. Dispose of it when you get back to shore.

Reduce, reuse, and recycle plastic. Try to find and use bags, packaging, and other items made of "green" plastic. This biodegradable plastic is made from cornstarch or other agricultural products. It decomposes over time.

According to David Helvarg, author of *50 Ways to Save the Ocean*, about 60 percent of trash left on beaches and 90 percent of trash found floating in the world's oceans is made up of plastic bags, food wrappers, bottles, fishing nets, fishing line, packing material, and balloons. (Many balloons released for special celebrations end up in the sea.) Helvarg says that the accumulation of everyday plastic in the ocean causes more damage than oil spills. Oil naturally dissolves over time. Plastic never does.

A study by the Algalita Marine Research Foundation found that parts of the North Pacific Ocean contain six times more plastic dust by weight than zooplankton, the basic fish food at the bottom of the marine food chain. Perhaps worse, fish often mistake pieces of plastic for food. They fill their stomachs with bits of plastic and starve. Pollutants absorbed by

You can help protect fish from plastic and other trash by leaving beaches cleaner than you find them. You can also participate in cleanups like this one in Miami Beach, Florida.

the plastic eventually poison such fish as tuna, billfish, and sharks. The toxins may also affect the reproduction and development of young fish and other marine organisms.

Avoid endangered and protected fish. Only fish for species that are plentiful in the ocean. If you accidentally catch the wrong kind of fish, release the fish without hurting it. When using live bait, use only species that already live in the fishery. Introducing foreign fish will upset the area's ecological balance.

Leave wildlife and its habitat undisturbed, including coral reefs and bird nests near fishing spots. If you notice damage or pollution caused by others, tell area authorities.

algae Aquatic organisms that have chlorophyll and other pigments and, like plants, make their own food through photosynthesis.

catch-and-release fishing The practice of returning fish to the water after hooking them.

channel marker A buoy with a distinctive color and shape that helps boats navigate federal waters.

conservationist Someone who works to protect animals, plants, and natural resources.

fishery A place where anglers can catch fish.

gill A fish's breathing organ.

jetty A structure, like a pier, built out into a body of water.

jetty creeper A safety sandal that has a rubber sole with metal spikes or cleats for traction.

latitude The distance north or south of the equator.

methylmercury A toxic compound of mercury.

nautical chart A graphic representation of a sea area and nearby coastal regions. It shows features such as depths of water, heights of land, navigational hazards, etc.

neoprene A type of synthetic rubber.

overfishing Fishing excessively; exhausting the supply of usable fish in an area.

pectoral fin The fin that lies just behind the gill opening on each side of a fish.

slurry A thin mixture of water and another material.

species A group of animals or plants that are similar and can produce offspring.

tide line The front edge of the moving water.

wake The path of waves caused by the movement of a boat through water.

American Sportfishing Association (ASA)
225 Reinekers Lane, Suite 420
Alexandria, VA 22314
(703) 519-9691
Web site: http://www.asafishing.org
The ASA represents the interests of sixty million American anglers and
the sportfishing industry. It addresses pending laws and policies
that could significantly affect the business or sport of fishing.

Canadian Parks and Wilderness Society (CPAWS)
506-250 City Centre Avenue
Ottawa, ON K1R 6K7
Canada
(800) 333-WILD [9453]
Web site: http://www.cpaws.org
This nonprofit conservation organization is devoted to protecting
Canada's wilderness heritage, including coastal and marine areas.

Coastal Conservation Association (CCA)
6919 Portwest, Suite 100
Houston, TX 77024
(800) 201-FISH [3474]
Web site: http://www.joincca.org
The CCA educates the public about conserving marine resources. It
also reviews fishery management and regulation issues under
consideration by federal agencies. It offers a youth membership
that includes a newsletter, T-shirt transfer, and fish stickers.

International Game Fish Association (IGFA)
300 Gulf Stream Way

Dania Beach, FL 33004

(954) 927-2628

Web site: http://www.igfa.org

The IGFA is an education and conservation organization. It is a recognized Coastal Ecosystem Learning Center that maintains members' worldwide fishing records and runs the IGFA Fishing Hall of Fame & Museum. The IGFA offers free Junior Angler events, videos, pro tips, games, and contests.

Living Oceans Society

P.O. Box 320

235 First Street

Sointula, BC V0N 3E0

Canada

(250) 973-6580

Web site: http://www.livingoceans.org

The Living Oceans Society is Canada's largest organization that focuses exclusively on marine conservation issues. It works to protect the British Columbia coastal ecosystem along Canada's Pacific coast.

National Coalition for Marine Conservation (NCMC)

4 Royal Street SE

Leesburg, VA 20175

(703) 777-0037

Web site: http://www.savethefish.org

The NCMC is a nonprofit group dedicated to conserving such saltwater fish as swordfish, marlin, shark, tuna, striped bass, menhaden, and herring. It brings together anglers and environmentalists to promote sustainable recreational and commercial fisheries.

Recreational Fishing Alliance (RFA)
P.O. Box 3080
New Gretna, NJ 08224
(888) 564-6732
Web site: http://www.joinrfa.org
The RFA is a political action organization that represents recreational anglers and the recreational fishing industry. It seeks to protect the rights of saltwater anglers and protect marine, boating, and tackle industry jobs. It also works to ensure sustainability of U.S. saltwater fisheries.

Stripers Forever
P.O. Box 2781
South Portland, ME 04116-2781
Web site: http://www.stripersforever.com
Stripers Forever is an Internet-based organization that seeks to have striped bass classified as a game fish. It seeks to end commercial exploitation of the species in favor of recreational fishing.

Web Sites

Due to the changing nature of Internet links, Rosen Publishing has developed an online list of Web sites related to the subject of this book. This site is updated regularly. Please use this link to access the list:

http:// www.rosenlinks.com/fish/salt

Adams, Aaron J. *Fly Fisherman's Guide to Saltwater Prey.* Mechanicsburg, PA: Stackpole Books, 2008.

Befus, Tyler. *A Kid's Guide to Flyfishing: It's More Than Catching Fish.* Boulder, CO: Johnson Books, 2007.

Bowman, Conway X. *The Orvis Guide to Beginning Saltwater Fly Fishing: 101 Tips for the Absolute Beginner.* New York, NY: Skyhorse Publishing, 2010.

Cottle, Samuel S. *In Danger at Sea: Adventures of a New England Fishing Family.* Camden, ME: Down East Books, 2007.

DeFelice, Cynthia C. *The Missing Manatee.* New York, NY: Farrar, Straus and Giroux, 2008.

Editors of *Popular Mechanics. How to Tempt a Fish: A Complete Guide to Fishing.* New York, NY: Hearst Books, 2008.

Labignan, Italo. *Hook, Line and Sinker: Everything Kids Want to Know About Fishing.* Toronto, Canada: Key Porter Books, 2007.

Lyons, Nick. *The Gigantic Book of Fishing Stories.* New York, NY: Skyhorse Publishing, 2007.

Pandolfi, Francis P., and Jono Pandolfi. *Spin Fishing Basics.* Short Hills, NJ: Burford Books, 2008.

Philbrick, W. R. *The Young Man and the Sea.* New York, NY: Blue Sky Press, 2004.

Ristori, Al. *The Complete Book of Surf Fishing.* New York, NY: Skyhorse Publishing, 2008.

Salas, Laura Purdie. *Saltwater Fishing.* Mankato, MN: Capstone Press, 2008.

Salisbury, Graham. *Lord of the Deep.* New York, NY: Delacorte Press, 2001.

Walker, Andrew D. *How to Improve at Fishing.* New York, NY: Crabtree Publishing Company, 2009.

Wilson, Geoff. *Geoff Wilson's Encyclopedia of Fishing Knots and Rigs.* Indianapolis, IN: Cardinal Publishers Group, 2008.

BIBLIOGRAPHY

American Heart Association. "Fish 101." May 20, 2010. Retrieved August 23, 2010 (http://www.heart.org/HEARTORG/GettingHealthy/NutritionCenter/Fish-101_UCM_305986_Article.jsp).

Barrett, Peter. *Fishing Soft Baits in Saltwater*. Short Hills, NJ: Burford Books, 2008.

Bryant, Charles W. "Introduction to How Seasickness Works." Discovery Health, 2010. Retrieved August 22, 2010 (http://health.howstuffworks.com/mental-health/neurological-conditions/seasickness.htm/printable).

Burnley, Eric B. *Fishing Saltwater Baits*. Short Hills, NJ: Burford Books, 2009.

Earle, Sylvia A. *The World Is Blue: How Our Fate and the Ocean's Are One*. Washington, DC: National Geographic, 2009.

Environmental Defense Fund. "Common Questions About Contaminants in Fish." March 17, 2010. Retrieved August 23, 2010 (http://www.edf.org/page.cfm?tagID=12667).

Fish4Fun.com. "Buoy Markers, Navigation and Waterway Boating Safety." 2010. Retrieved September 10, 2010 (http://www.fish4fun.com/buoys.htm).

Florida Sea Grant. "Catch-and-Release: Things You Can Do to Help Saltwater Fish Survive." May 2008. Retrieved August 24, 2010 (http://catchandrelease.org/Catch_and_Release_web.pdf).

Helvarg, David. *50 Ways to Save the Ocean*. Makawao, HI: Inner Ocean Publishing, 2006.

Pollizotto, Martin. *Saltwater Fishing Made Easy*. Camden, ME: International Marine/McGraw-Hill, 2006.

Ray, Daniel. "How to Use a Sabiki Rig to Catch Baitfish." eHow.com, 2010. Retrieved September 18, 2010 (http://www.ehow.com/how_4556170_use-sabiki-rig-catch-baitfish.html).

Schultz, Ken. *Ken Schultz's Essentials of Fishing: The Only Guide You Need to Catch Freshwater and Saltwater Fish*. Hoboken, NJ: John Wiley & Sons, 2010.

Shook, Michael D. *The Complete Idiot's Guide to Fly Fishing*. 2nd ed. New York, NY: Alpha Books, 2005.

U.S. Coast Guard Boating Safety Division. "Boating Under the Influence Initiatives." Boating Safety Resource Center, April 29, 2009. Retrieved September 11, 2010 (http://www.uscgboating.org/safety/boating_under_the_influence_initiatives.aspx).

U.S. Food and Drug Administration and U.S. Environmental Protection Agency. "What You Need to Know About Mercury in Fish and Shellfish." November 2009. Retrieved August 23, 2010 (http://water.epa.gov/scitech/swguidance/fishshellfish/outreach/upload/2004_05_24_fish_MethylmercuryBrochure.pdf).

Williams, Erik, and Malia Schwartz. "Catch-and-Release Fishing." Rhode Island Sea Grant. Retrieved September 12, 2010 (http://seagrant.gso.uri.edu/factsheets/catch-release_fs.html).

Winter, Allison. "Obama Admin Looks to Cast a Line with Anglers." NYTimes.com, April 16, 2010. Retrieved September 23, 2010 (http://www.nytimes.com/gwire/2010/04/16/16greenwire-obama-admin-looks-to-cast-a-line-with-anglers-95055.html?pagewanted=all).

World Fishing Network. "Gulf Fishery and Potential Lead Ban Update." WFN.tv, September 15, 2010. Retrieved September 20, 2010 (http://www.wfn.tv/news/oil-spill/video.php?video=409921).

World Fishing Network. "Major Fish Kill in Bayou Chaland." WFN.tv, September 15, 2010. Retrieved September 20, 2010 (http://www.wfn.tv/news/oil-spill/article.php?blog=409906).

INDEX

About the Author

Mary-Lane Kamberg is a professional writer who has published six books for children, including five Rosen titles. She is coleader of the Kansas City Writers Group and a member of the Midwest Children's Authors Guild. She loves the water and has spent a lot of time swimming, boating, and fishing. Her husband, Ken Kamberg, used to use poppers to fish for weakfish off the south shore of Long Island, New York.

About the Consultant

Benjamin Cowan has more than twenty years of both freshwater and saltwater angling experience. In addition to being an avid outdoorsman, Cowan is a member of many conservation organizations. He currently resides in west Tennessee.

Photo Credits

Cover, pp. 1, 3 © www.istockphoto.com/Bob Ingelhart; pp. 5, 39 Courtesy of Take Me Fishing; p. 8 Comstock/Thinkstock; p. 11 U.S. Coast Guard; pp. 14, 20, 21, 25, 41 Ron Brooks; pp. 15, 26, 29, 36 Shutterstock; p. 18 David De Lossy/Photodisc/Thinkstock; p. 23 Jetta Productions/Iconica/Getty Images; p. 30 Bob Reichenfeld/Dorling Kindersley/Getty Images; p. 32 © Pacific Stock/SuperStock; p. 33 Steve Winter/National Geographic/Getty Images; p. 43 istockphoto/Thinkstock; pp. 45, 50 (2 photos) © AP Images; p. 48 © Ko Sasaki/The New York Times/Redux; p. 54 © Jeff Greenberg/Photo Edit; back cover and interior graphics (silhouette) © www.istockphoto.com/A-Digit (green grass) © www.istockphoto.com/Makhnach M; (waves) © www.istockphoto.com/Michael Jay.

Designer: Nicole Russo; Editor: Andrea Sclarow;
Photo Researcher: Marty Levick